Pebble

Dogs

Shih Tzus

by Joanne Linden

Consulting Editor: Gail Saunders-Smith, PhD

Consultant: Jennifer Zablotny, DVM
Member, American Veterinary Medical Association

Capstone
press

Mankato, Minnesota

Pebble Books are published by Capstone Press,
151 Good Counsel Drive, P.O. Box 669, Mankato, Minnesota 56002.
www.capstonepress.com

1 2 3 4 5 6 11 10 09 08 07 06

Library of Congress Cataloging-in-Publication Data
Linden, Joanne.
    Shih tzus / by Joanne Linden.
    p. cm. — (Pebble. Dogs)
    Includes bibliographical references and index.
    ISBN-13: 978-0-7368-6328-5 (hardcover)
    ISBN-10: 0-7368-6328-1 (hardcover)
    1. Shih tzu—Juvenile literature. I. Title. II. Series: Pebble Books. Dogs.
SF429.S64L55 2007
636.76—dc22   2005037364

Summary: Simple text and photographs introduce the Shih tzu breed, its
growth from puppy to adult, and pet care information.

Note to Parents and Teachers

The Dogs set supports national science standards related to life
science. This book describes and illustrates Shih tzus. The images
support early readers in understanding the text. The repetition of
words and phrases helps early readers learn new words. This book
also introduces early readers to subject-specific vocabulary words,
which are defined in the Glossary section. Early readers may need
assistance to read some words and to use the Table of Contents,
Glossary, Read More, Internet Sites, and Index sections of the book.

Table of Contents

Shih tzu   (sheet zoo)

Lion Dog

Shih tzu means "lion dog" in Chinese.
The first shih tzus came from China.

Long hair covers shih tzu
bodies. It even grows
on their faces.
The fur is thick
like a lion's mane.

Shih tzus once lived
in palaces. They were pets
of kings and queens.
These fancy dogs
like being spoiled.

From Puppy to Adult

Shih tzu puppies
come in many colors.
They can be gold, black,
or a mix of colors.

Shih tzu puppies grow into adults that look happy and proud. They wag their furry tails above their backs.

Shih Tzu Care

Shih tzus with long hair must be brushed each day. Owners tie bows to keep hair out of dogs' eyes.

Some shih tzus have
short haircuts.
Their owners take them
to a groomer every month.

Shih tzus need clean water and dog food every day. They might need their beards brushed after they eat!

Shih tzus shouldn't be in hot sun or cold snow. They love to play outside on a nice day.

Glossary

beard—hair that grows around the mouth and chin

China—a country in Asia

groomer—a trained worker who washes and trims the hair and nails of dogs

mane—long, thick hair that grows on the head and neck of some animals like lions and horses

palace—a grand home for kings and queens

Read More

Soy, Teri. *Shih Tzus.* Popular Dog Library. Philadelphia: Chelsea House, 1999.

Temple, Bob. *Shih Tzus.* Dogs. Edina, Minn.: Abdo, 2000.

Internet Sites

FactHound offers a safe, fun way to find Internet sites related to this book. All of the sites on FactHound have been researched by our staff.

Here's how:

1. Visit *www.facthound.com*
2. Choose your grade level.
3. Type in this book ID **0736863281** for age-appropriate sites. You may also browse subjects by clicking on letters, or by clicking on pictures and words.
4. Click on the **Fetch It** button.

FactHound will fetch the best sites for you!

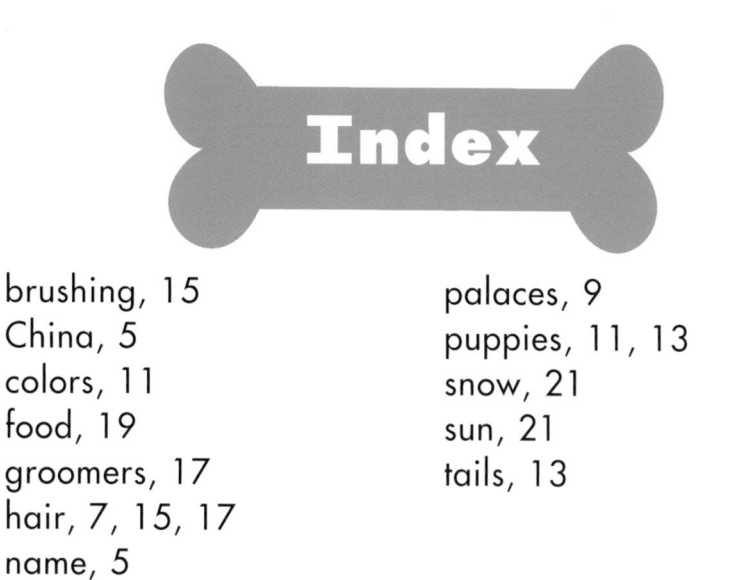

Index

Word Count: 162
Grade: 1
Early-Intervention Level: 14

Editorial Credits

Heather Adamson, editor; Juliette Peters, set designer; Ted Williams, book designer; Kelly Garvin, photo researcher/photo editor

Photo Credits

Capstone Press/Karon Dubke, 8, 14, 16, 18
Cheryl A. Ertelt, 12
Norvia Behling, 4, 6, 10
PhotoEdit Inc./Robin Nelson, 20
Ron Kimball Stock/Ron Kimball, 1
Superstock/age fotostock, cover